CONTENT:

FOREWORD BY RAYMOND AARON

Beyond the Tour, What you Really Need to Know about Senior Living Facilities is a comprehensive guide for those who are on this journey, searching for a senior living community for themselves, for their loved ones or for friends. People who want to understand the foundations of the senior living world must read this book. It offers straightforward, easy-to-understand insights to this ever- evolving segment of health care, which otherwise often can be confusing and frustrating. The information, advice and several free bonuses offered in this book are designed to save readers from costly detours and delays during the search for the perfect community.

As an entrepreneur and teacher, I know that it takes a great deal of experience, at every level of a particular industry, to become a true expert at the level Jo Letwaitis proves to be. She is here for you, regardless of where you are on your path and your search because she **really** understands first-hand how difficult, frustrating and emotionally taxing this exercise can be for individuals.

As publisher, I am pleased to welcome Jo Letwaitis into our library of outstanding experts dedicated to helping others by offering their knowledge and experience. It is our hope that this book will help you turn a difficult process into one is positive and rewarding as she provides you with assistance along each step of the way.

CHAPTER ONE – WHAT DO ALL THE ACRONYMS MEAN?

There are so many different 'types' of senior living organizations, each with its own amenities and levels of care. Once merely called retirement homes, these communities have become quite specific. Although not discussed at length in this book, these can include shared housing, group homes, community-based residential facilities, senior housing and retirement communities. The discussion here involves the most common types, but this list is by no means exhaustive.

1 INDEPENDENT LIVING (IL)

Independent living is just that – **independent** living or living on one's own. These communities are called by this name because they don't offer, as part of the monthly rent, services to assist you with your daily activities. These activities of daily life, by definition, include the essential actions you complete over the course of the day and night to take care of your own basic needs. These include bathing, grooming, dressing, eating, toileting and being able to navigate your surroundings without assistance.

Think of a senior retirement community, meant for those older than age 55, where you come and go as you please, tend to your own needs, and even possibly still drive a car. For an additional cost, certain optional services can be added like the availability of a meal plan where you can choose to eat meals their services provide between two and three meals a day. In these plans, breakfast is usually served at a buffet and offered at no additional charge. Transportation can be arranged when you need to get you to your appointments. A hair salon may be on the premises, along with other resort-like amenities like a health club, tennis courts and/or swimming pool.

Certain independent living communities offer the added benefit of keeping their residents in their apartments a wee bit longer in an attempt to keep them from moving out and into an Assisted Living facility where additional services are available. Some of these medical and therapy services may possibly be covered by health insurance policies if a physician provides a prescription or order for them. Physical therapy, occupational therapy, speech therapy and home health care are among the services offered through third party subcontractors working with the Independent Living companies. Savvier companies such as Brookdale have incorporated those 'added services' into a division of their parent company so they can keep more of the profits in their own pockets.

While on the subject of this second layer of services, please be aware that there is a huge difference between home health care and home care. The first provides 'health assistance' and is often covered by insurance while the latter, home care, is more companion-driven and is funded by private payment.

You will see later in this chapter a term called CCRC, or Continuing Care Retirement Community. Independent Living is the first 'level' of this continuum and is one which allows you to age in place and move throughout the campus into the higher levels, depending on your care needs. But, I digress.

If you are an adult child of someone looking to downsize (or who needs to downsize), this is an excellent first step. While maintaining as much independence as possible, services can be purchased, as the need arises.

2 ASSISTED LIVING (AL)

Assisted living is the 'next up' development in aging. Each state has a Department of Public Health which regulates these communities. Here in Illinois it is:

TITLE 77: PUBLIC HEALTH, CHAPTER I: DEPARTMENT OF PUBLIC HEALTH; SUBCHAPTER c: LONG-TERM CARE FACILITIES; PART 295 ASSISTED LIVING AND SHARED HOUSING ESTABLISHMENT CODE http://www.ilga.gov/commission/jcar/ad mincode/077/07700295sections.html

Assisted living is just that – assistance available for daily living activities like bathing, dressing, grooming, toileting and/or walking (ambulating). Because of regulations, there are certain things that will occur when you request this level of care, First, a representative from the assisted living community will assess a potential resident to make certain that person can perform specific skills such as standing, walking, pivoting from bed to chair and the like. If the person requires total assistance for more than two daily living activities, he or she will be deemed inappropriate for acceptance to an assisted living facility.

Be wary of the senior living community that says, "No problem; we can do this with x, y and z." Ask them to share with you the state guidelines to determine where you or your loved one fits into the equation. A good company will be able to do that. A great company will not only be able to do that, but also will have the courage to say that they cannot care for your loved one -- but **CAN** help you find a place that is able to do so!

3 MEMORY CARE (ALZ)

Memory care comes in all shapes and sizes. Some places have cute names for this area, floor, wing or section of a building. Some of these names include "Circle of friends," "neighborhood," and the dreaded "locked unit," which, surprisingly, always has a painted mural on the entry door.

To understand memory care and what each particular community has to offer, you need to start at the beginning.

Differences exist between types of memory loss. There is the normal forgetfulness that can accompany aging. Then there is a diagnosis of one of the more than thirty types of dementia. Finally, there is a diagnosis of Alzheimer's disease. Do you remember learning in grade school math that a square is always a rectangle, but a rectangle is not always a square? Similarly, Alzheimer's is always dementia, but not all dementia is Alzheimer's! Keep this in mind because the varying paths this disease travels is important when choosing a memory care community – which is a community that cares for those with memory issues specifically as opposed to one that has a 'wing' or 'section' within the building or on the campus. Again, in Illinois, communities licensed for assisted living that also have a memory care component must complete additional licensure documentation for the "Alzheimer's Disclosure" level, IL 295.4060. This documentation is a series of policies and procedures that identify how someone with dementia will be cared for, what those requirements and restrictions entail and all staffing and training requirements, in addition to a plethora of other very detailed programming policies.

While searching for this type of community, it is imperative to be absolutely truthful about your loved one's disease level. Imagine how you would feel if you did not inform the community about the person's tendency to wander and then received a midnight call that informs you that person is missing!

4 SKILLED NURSING FACILITY (SNF)

A skilled nursing facility is just that – one where skilled nursing care is required. Normally, two paths are included in a skilled nursing care facility: rehab, or short term care; and long term care. Many seniors will be transferred or discharged from a hospitalization to a SNF. Be aware: you have a **choice** of skilled nursing facilities; THIS IS IMPORTANT to keep in mind. You also have a choice as to the length of stay. Sorry SNF owners/readers. The fact is that quite often SNF operators like to keep their patients for that famous 100 day stay covered by Medicare.

Skilled Nursing Facilities are unique animals. If this is the level of care your loved one needs, I highly recommend consulting a few great websites to learn more about them:

1. www.**medicare**.gov/coverage/**skille d-nursing**-facility-care.html
2. http://www.medicareinteractive.or g/page2.php?topic=counselor&pag e=case_study&casestudy_id=18
3. https://www.**medicare**.gov/Pubs/p df/10153.pdf

Don't fall into the trap of having to stay in skilled care for the 100 days. Learn about your benefits.

5 SUPPORTIVE LIVING FACILITY (SLF)

Supportive living is a phenomenal development within assisted living. By definition, supportive living is an alternative to nursing home care for low income older persons and persons with disabilities under Medicaid.

By combining apartment-style housing with personal care and other services, residents can live independently and take part in the decision-making process. Supportive living emphasizes personal choice, dignity, privacy and individuality. The Department of Healthcare and Family Services obtains a "waiver" to allow for payment for services that are not routinely covered by Medicaid. These services include personal care, homemaking, laundry, medication supervision, social activities, recreation and 24-hour staff to meet both the residents' scheduled and unscheduled needs. The resident is responsible for paying the cost of room and board at the facility. (Source: http://www.slfillinois.com/)

However, these facilities are also considered "AL-light," meaning that their residency requirements are not of the same as those for assisted living communities. (More information about this can be found at: http://www.slfillinois.com/factsheetresident.html, and http://www.ilga.gov/commission/jcar/admincode/089/089001460B02300R.html.) To be considered for a SLF, you cannot have any diagnosed or undiagnosed memory care issues. While a wonderful concept that a few companies in Illinois implement well, this care is based strictly on the financial ability to pay; therefore, there is often a waiting list.

6 CONTINUING CARE RETIREMENT COMMUNITY (CCRC)

Here everything is available on one campus: Independent Living, Assisted Living, Memory Care and Skilled Nursing. Many CCRCs require an entrance fee which can range as high as $450,000; this amount may be fully or partially refundable when the apartment is resold.

For those who can afford a CCRC, it has many benefits -- like options for an active life-style, life-enriching programs, all the comforts of home, and then some. However, there are also drawbacks. If the time comes, for example, couples may not be allowed to live together should one require a higher level of care. The impaired partner will be asked to move to another building where appropriate care is provided.

Don't fall for the line, "You don't have to move away; we are all on the same grounds." The fact is you **will** have to move. The surroundings will be completely different, as will be the staff.

Imagine someone with dementia leaving familiar surroundings and going into another setting. Will they understand that they've gone just down the hall, down the elevator, across the parking lot or into another building? Even though the person may still remain close to where they were, do they understand that -- or do they sense they're being removed and relocated somewhere else?

As a note of caution, the concept above just does not pertain to CCRCs; some AL/ALZ communities do this same thing – provide two separate buildings that offer two separate levels of care.

BONUS 1: Visit my website to download your free copy of "The Guide to Choosing a Senior Living Community," www.beyondtheseniorlivingtour.com.

CHAPTER TWO – AND IT GOES LIKE THIS

When you set out to search, one of the first places you probably turn to is the internet. In this day and age of technology, everyone has links and you may quickly get lost in all the pages. Without realizing it, you may have signed up to as many as 10 different services, all set to help you find that perfect place.

1 SOMEHOW, YOU FIND YOURSELF ON THE RECEIVING END OF A PHONE CALL

When you set out to search for a community, the most natural thing to do is access the internet. BE CAREFUL! There are so many services out. First in this range are the horrid, who 'spray and pray' -- meaning they don't really listen. They just plug in your info, then send it out, shotgun style, to at least 30 places, and pray that one of them will be good enough for you so they will receive a referral fee. Then there are the decent, smaller, privately-owned companies who work with local, well-informed and respected consultants.

2 TO SET UP A TOUR

When you take that call and start answering all their questions, you find they want to be the ones to ask some, if not all, the questions. You see, there is usually one reason, and one reason alone, they make that call to you. That reason is to set up a tour. The community has different statistical measures to show performance in the following categories: phone call inquiry to tour; tour to deposit; tour to move in and so forth. Their goal during that phone call is often different than your goal. Your goal is to see what they have to offer while their goal is get you in the door.

3 WHAT ARE THE RATES, FEES, and COSTS?

Of course, with all services and rentals, you don't want to waste anyone's time –

yours, theirs, and the time of others who may be interested in accompanying you on this tour. I have had as many as eight family members touring at the same time. Imagine the scheduling nightmare that created for them.

What are the rates? Any fees? Costs involved? Sharpen your pencil because there are so many different pricing models out there, after you have visited two or three, they all begin to blur. Because some communities are 'all inclusive' while others are so customized -- right down to the number of medications that need to be administered, you will not truly understand or remember the differences. I'll break this down for you in an upcoming chapter.

Be satisfied that you are given a range of costs over the phone, however, don't put the cart before the horse. Keep in mind that you may not even care for the place, so don't get worked up by the lack of information you receive over the phone from the Community Sales and Marketing Director. It truly is best to experience the place before getting into all that.

Prior to setting up a tour, you should insist on securing at least this information:

1. What are the apartment choices and sizes?
2. What are the costs for those different apartment choices and sizes?
3. Under which licensure does the community operate? Again, depending on the state, check with the state department of health for related information.
4. Is there an RN or LPN there, on the premises who is awake and responsible for care 24/7? That answer should be YES.

5. What is the caregiver to resident ratio? If each caregiver has a load of less than 10 residents, that is good.

4 WE NEED MORE INFORMATION FROM YOU!

If you are just shopping, which is fine to do, make sure the sales and marketing person knows that. Most communities respect your timeline. And, yes -- give them your real email address to allow them to keep you informed of any changes, specials events taking place. These marketing people have certain quotas to meet, such as number of calls to make per week and appointments to set. However, I have learned that speaking with these individuals is much better than speaking with the large referral agencies and, if you develop a decent working relationship, they will be more respectful of you and your concerns.

5 DATE SET TO TOUR – WHAT TO EXPECT

It is always a good idea, if possible, to schedule your tour for either mid-morning or a time closest to dinner, say around 4 p.m. The mid-morning visit should provide you with a snapshot of how the community engages residents in activities and of the various settings – both those of quiet enjoyment and of hustle and bustle. If you visit around 2 p.m., chances are things will be quieter as, considering lunch normally is the largest meal of the day, residents may be napping in their rooms or, hopefully, involved in one of the different nooks and crannies available for solitude, reading or visiting.

Regardless of where you go, an overarching routine exists for any senior's daily life. In the morning, caregivers help residents begin their day, assisting them with bathing, toilet use, groom and dress. After this, those who need to be escorted to the dining room are assisted; others will amble there on their own. Look out for those communities with a strict breakfast time and an unwavering commitment to uphold it. My mother, who was a night owl and loved to dance, would have laughed if you tried to wake her at 6 a.m. so she could eat by 8 a.m. Why would anyone try to change her lifestyle at age 80? The same concept applies to your loved one, but I will discuss this more later.

Mornings also include medication administration that, if done correctly, follow some privacy guidelines. Outside services -- services that exist onsite but are separately owned and/or operated, such as physical or occupational therapy -- can also be offered and/or performed at any time during the day. From 11 a.m. until 1 p.m., while lunch is being prepared and served, other caregiving activity is taking place. After lunch, attendance to the resident's activities of daily living

(ADLs), and provide either some quiet time or other activities. Note: The levels and types of activities available are quite dependent on the level of care provided at that particular community. You would not expect a "Lunch Bunch" -- where a group of residents head out to a local restaurant – to exist in a skilled nursing facility, or expect residents to be involved in a huge, wall-sized crossword puzzle at a memory care community.

After dinner is also a good time to tour -- or at least drop in to see what happens when the management team leaves for the day. Are all the residents plunked down in front of a television set, or is some type of engagement still taking place? This is not to say that television is bad. In fact, that may be the resident's past modus operandi to watch the news and relax after dinner. However, this activity shouldn't be forced on all residents. Thinking back to my childhood, my dad would relax in his lounge chair and watch the news after dinner while my mother would get ready to go ballroom dancing with my aunts. They truly exemplified two extremes under one roof.

6 YOUR TOUR -- WHAT DID YOU LEARN ABOUT THE FACILITY?

It is imperative to note what you learn from each tour. What is your takeaway? What did you want answered when you got there?

This tour, or at least the tours I personally conduct, go like this:

The visitor is introduced to the sales and marketing director or to me and is then escorted into a private office or dining room. After some formalities, I ask what occurrences led to this particular step. Some folks just start the ball rolling early without any particular impetus for the tour at this time, however many have a profound response. Some of these responses may be:

- My mother was found wandering outside in the middle of the night.
- A neighbor saw my dad about a mile away from home without a coat on.
- My dad fell and is hospitalized, but is being discharged tomorrow and the doctor said he cannot return home alone.

I want the story to unfold as each family member present tells me about their loved one. I listen, as skillfully as I can, to each person's story and stay focused on their needs. This isn't a conversation per se, but is a gently guided tale of the person and his or her immediate requirements, as well as the daily needs that will allow the person to continue to live as the person they are! Once the story is completed, I ask if they would like to know about a few things we can offer that tap directly into the needs I just learned. (Some folks in the industry call this process "discovery" – but I feel the discovery is for the community. Therefore, I'm torn about the use of that word. In my view, it's not about the community, but about the senior we are attempting to help.)

I ask if I can provide them with some of our literature after we walk through the building -- or if this is a focal point now. It is their choice. It is **always** the family's choice. Then, I ask if they would like to see the community. Once up and out of the private space, I keep what they told me in mind. I do not conduct cookie-cutter tours. You know the ones that point out, "Here's the dining room and here's the living room. Over there's the library." Rather, I prefer to customize the tour to showcase the community and highlight the areas and features that will best meet their loved ones needs.

While a consultant, I once followed a tour at one of the 'big box' companies. This company prides itself with trying to become the biggest, however not necessarily the best. Anyway, as I tagged along, the sales person was very excited to point out the bar and continuously stressed that their residents loved, just loved the "Happy Hour." The organization was trying to make happy hour a daily occurrence, serving real liquor -- if permitted by the physician. I just saw the enthusiasm drain out of one poor lady as she turned to the sales and marketing gal and said, 'My mother is a recovering alcoholic, and I don't think it would be a good idea for her to be in this environment.' That was the end of that sale. Hmm, I wondered. What did the sales person get wrong? Did she really listen to the woman's story of her mom prior to the tour?

To complete my tours, we return to the office and I ask questions that will get me a 'no' as a response. Now, that's not what you think. I want to reveal any objections and answer questions we I can determine how we can best meet this potential resident's needs. When I hear "no" in answer to the question, "Can you think of any reason why you your loved one wouldn't be an excellent fit?" or something along those lines, I know that I've done my job correctly. That is the time we can move on to the next step.

CHAPTER THREE- CHECKLIST OF THE FIVE SENSES

The literature and website can take you only so far. What you truly need to do is go and visit -- physically look, listen, smell and feel the environment for yourself.

1 LOOK AND SEE

Arrive at the building approximately 15 minutes prior to the set appointment time and see who greets you. Let the greeter know that you are early and ask if there is a bathroom you could use prior to your appointment. Get lost. Check out a few details. Most places disguise hand rails as lovely extended chair rail detailing;

these are actually a great receptacle for used tissues, gum and small bits of trash.

How do the residents you encounter look? Do they have "bed head" hair, or are they appropriately groomed, wearing clean clothing and having fresh faces?

What about the carpeting, the hung wall art, the fake plants (ugh!) or other knick knacks? Are they appropriate? Are they clean?

A good friend and colleague, Jennifer Prell, founder and owner of Elderwerks -- a senior living referral service here in Illinois, shared with me a comprehensive check list. With her permission, the checklist is included in the back of this book under resources.

2 FEEL THE ENERGY (OR NOT)

What did you immediately sense when you walked into the building? I always ask that questions of families with whom I tour because it is important to know how they are feeling. Can they picture their loved one or themselves living here?

All developers want to be ahead of the curve when it comes to design – but a few have seriously missed the mark because they catered to the adult children rather than to the senior residents themselves. I often hear people say, "I can see myself living here, but my mom is more" traditional, more simple, more old-fashioned (or more fill-in-the-blank) "and she would think this is too grand for her." This is very true while we are still serving the "Greatest Generation," which includes those who have lived through several wars and the Great Depression. When it comes to the "Baby Boomers," that's a whole other story! Where's the martini bar? Where's the wine tasting or soaking tub, the day spa? You can fill in the blank.

What you sense when you walk in the door is **vital** to the equation. Does the place feel loving and nurturing or does it feel cold and sterile? You know your loved one best. What do you think they will enjoy most?

3 SMELL THE DIFFERENT PARTS OF THE BUILDINGS

Different sections of the building may hold different smells. Ask if there's an area where the third-party care providers (the home health care staff, the hospice staff, podiatrists and physicians which come in to see residents, but are not on staff) treat patients. Does it smell differently than the other areas?

How about the dining room or bistro? Do pleasant smells waft from the kitchen? Do they remind you of meal times at home?

How do the residents smell? Do they seem bathed or unkempt? There are certain times, usually before or immediately following meals, when a resident may have an "accident," or, when you pass the room of a resident, you may smell something foul. However, these odors are somewhat normal. You should ask the staff when they help residents use the bathroom facilities who are in need of this routine. I have found that if a care giver follows the Individualized Service Plan (ISP), that person will have a good sense when residents need to go to the bathroom. The staff should have this routine as part of the resident's daily routine to avoid accidents.

Ask to visit not only the model room, but also an actual resident's room. Many residents are proud of their surroundings and offer their suite as a model . Don't ask for a vacant room. Ask to peek into a room when a resident isn't currently present. This is very likely, particularly since the concept of assisted living is to provide socialization; a resident truly isn't 'living' in his room, but within the community.

By going into, or at the very least, stepping foot across the threshold of an occupied room, you will t experience what a typical resident's room smells like. It should smell fresh, clean and welcoming rather than dark, musty and dirty.

Also ask to visit the laundry room. What does it smell like? What does it look like?

4 TASTE THEIR FOOD

Assisted living and memory care communities are turning the corner on the dining service. There is much to be said about the dining experience. As we age, dining becomes a focal part of our day. How many times have you thought about dinner during the course of your day? Many residents consider lunch the pivotal part of their day.

The food should be nutritious, not outrageous. The management company or 'operator of the building' needs to take into account the demographics of the community it is serving rather than have an 'across the board' mentality within their buildings. For example, poached salmon with herbs and wild rice pilaf, a salad on the side, served along with poached pears and a brandy cream sauce would be wonderful for someone living in the Pacific Northwest, but someone in the south suburbs of Chicago may not prefer this style of cooking. I once argued the point of 'coursing' a meal. The company providing the food wanted beautifully printed menus and the meal served with the salad and bread first, then the entrée, then the dessert. This is a beautiful concept for assisted living and for those that ate like that earlier in their lifetime. However, the issue with this particular community was that it was mainly mid-to-late stage memory care. These folks were able to appreciate the beauty of a placard that showed the foods, but would most likely attempt to eat the 's sample plate' and may not have the --- ability or attention span any longer to get through the courses.

Having said that, request to have a meal there. Don't ask for lunch -- ask for dinner! The largest meal is lunch. It would be beneficial for you to experience what the resident experiences at dinner time. Hopefully, you are pleasantly surprised.

If your loved one needs memory care, ask about finger foods. What and how are these served? Is soup a mainstay? Does anyone remember 'fish sticks' and frozen French fries for dinner on Friday evening? Are all the items frozen, then placed on cookie sheets and stuck in the oven? Are they served with lots of ketchup to make them tolerable? We've come a long way, baby. Observe and taste what's being served at dinner. Enjoy your meal.

5 HEAR THE SOUNDS

You should hear the soft sounds of workers, offering one-on-one care, as well as the louder, uplifting sounds of activities. Joyfulness should be the overarching sense in the common areas. Listen for any small, quieter utterances of 'help' or 'miss, can you help me' or for soft, repetitive moaning. If you hear any of these sounds, observe whether or not the caregiving staff responds to these pleas.

The sounds will differ a bit if you're investigating a memory care community or a section of the assisted living building that cares for those with memory care issues. Be mindful that this level of care offers challenges that may not be obvious to someone not accustomed to the specific matters of dementia-related diseases.

6 IMAGINE YOURSELF

Can you imagine yourself being your loved one and living in this environment? As I've mentioned elsewhere in this book, many assisted living community developers are a bit ahead of the curve and have designed elements to suit the 'next generation.' Therefore, they have left little to which the current generation can relate.

Perhaps the structure is a bit too grandiose. Its two story foyers and grand staircases or modern furniture may withstand the wear of time, but lack the traditional designs that offer the Greatest Generation some familiarity and identification. I've heard folks say, "Yup, this is **me** all over the place, but my mother wouldn't think she's 'good enough' for this style." I've seen Frank Lloyd Wright-inspired properties built in geographic areas where farms once stood meant intend to care for those that either grew up working or owning the farm. Their owners don't understand why they're half empty. The reality is the buildings just don't fit the backgrounds or identities of the senior market they want to target.

Aside from the physical design, do you think your loved one will feel comfortable amongst the settings? Is there a fireplace? Are there nooks and crannies in which to grab a book or a puzzle or just have some solitude? Are card tables always set up or does one have to seek them out when they want to play?

What are the other residents like? Have you gone up to one or two of them and introduced yourself? Try that. Does the person respond positively or do they grasp the opportunity to say something negative?

By the time you've used all your senses on this tour, you'll have a better feeling about whether or not this place makes sense for your loved one and family.

CHAPTER FOUR – SO ALL'S GOOD, RIGHT?

When I first started out in the senior living world, I was quite naive about ownerships, management companies, Real Estate Investment Trusts (REITS) that invest monies into these projects, operators and privately held companies. I had no idea that one, single, stand-alone community may be owned and managed by as many as four different entities and was amazed to find that that is often the case.

Initially, there is an owner, the person who initially purchased the physical property along with the business. That person might later obtain a private investor to help fund this purchase. Together, they may hire a management company to actually manage the day-to-day operations. While the nuances are subtle, this structure is important to understand for a number of reasons.

Some of the reasons are listed a bit later, but imagine this. The last company I worked with retained the same owners, but the management company they contracted with was acquired by another company; later on, that second management company switched companies. Because of that, the direction, vision and goals of the company switched three times just within six months.

1 WHO REALLY OWNS THE COMPANY? AGAIN, WHAT HAPPENS IF THEY SELL?

This can get incredibly confusing for consumers as well as for the staff. It is critical to understand and know who **really** owns the company and who manages it. To do this, you must ask questions about both. Learn when, how and why the company was acquired and if the owners are the operators; this means asking if the owners actually **manage** the community you are visiting.

If the answer is no, the community is managed by a 'management company,' you want to find out who that company is, how long it has been in business in the STATE IN WHICH THE COMMUNITY EXISTS, and how many other communities it manages and for which it provides the same level of care. For example, a company may operate out of Florida, but has other communities in Illinois. If it specializes in independent and assisted living, but the place you tour in Illinois is a memory care-specific community, be wary! That's an instant, "Uh-oh!" I reiterate: UH-OH! Does this company and its staff have the experience and knowledge to translate, uphold and defend the specific state regulations for Illinois? Sadly, the answer is often no. Some management companies look only for the business revenue aspect when they decide to 'go after' the business, rather than care about the human aspect of the business. Therefore, they may not be aware of the level of care offered at that location nor have any inkling as to the state rules that regulate the business.

Does their regional team (usually resident care, operations and sales/marketing) have experience with the level of care offered at this community? Have members of this team ever visited the state? This comment may be considered somewhat tongue in cheek, but there's a reason to ask. From a marketing standpoint, do the company and their team understand the local culture? Do they understand the area from which you will hire most of your staff? More importantly, do they understand the area(s) in which most of their **residents** and **families** were raised or grew up?

Also consider what happens when the owners sell or change management companies? Understand that, even in the best-oiled transitional plan, there will be changes. However, often, to what extent those changes occur is a mystery. Why did you choose this community? Was it because of the executive director or the resident care director? Well, if the new management company brings in 'one of their own,' this will create another 'get to know you' opportunity. Did you choose this community because you thought the rates were appropriate or reasonable? Within six to 12 months, the new management company will most likely revisit all contracts and potentially change rates, services, staff ratios, vendors and care providers. When you negotiate your contract, try and get some of these details worked through or obtain a guarantee to carry you're your current agreement for at least within the first two years should changes take place.

2 HOW DOES THE STAFF RECEIVE TRAINING?

When my previous consulting business provided placement assistance, I made certain that my clients understood the particular state training regulations; yes, regulations exist that offer guidance about staff training. You must make certain that the community that interests you follows those guidelines and, hopefully, exceeds them.

Key questions you need answered include:

1. What are the guidelines for staff training?
2. How does the staff receive that training?
3. What does that staff training consist of?
4. Did the last state survey require any additional training?
5. Did that training occur? If so, can I see an example of the curriculum used?
6. Does the company pay for the staff to receive training?

3 HOW MUCH TRAINING AND REGARDING WHAT?

Every senior community will tell you that they train their staff members; however, you also must ask the question, "Regarding what?" For the purpose of this discussion, I will focus on the care staff -- usually the largest department within the community. However **ALL** staff need to be trained to assist the care staff and also **must** be cardiopulmonary resuscitation (CPR)-certified! This cross-training is extremely important since there are many different components involved in conducting a successful training program. Although I am certain that each employee goes through a routine interview, a post-offer physical, a background investigation (which I will discuss more shortly) and a general orientation, but you need to find out what happens after that.

Some state regulations direct the community regarding how many staff training hours are needed. Others will just offer a vague statement about annual training.

A successful training program -- one that provides multilevel staff training, should include not only the 'direct resident care' components like how to assist residents with daily living activities, but also provides specific training related to the level of care involved in the area in which they work.

For example, if a community specializes in assisted living, staff members should be trained about the specifics involved in the different levels of assistance required for **each** resident. It is not sufficient to offer only general training in this area since individual residents have specific needs. Because one may require incontinence care, the entire staff should understand the importance of a bathroom routine, the types of incontinence products that may be used, what the skin should look like during the time that person assists with care and any precautions required, as well as what to do if skin looks abnormal. Just as important, the staff needs to know how to respond to the resident throughout each part of the care. They need to be aware that how they speak to the resident from start to finish is extremely important. Consider this: This is **only one type of care**, incontinence! What about bathing, dressing, grooming, or escorting residents to the dining area? How about assisting them with eating, encouraging their participation in activities (whether the participation will be active or passive), or providing them with individualized attention? Remember the Individualized Service Plan (ISP)?

Understand also that training should not end with resident care. Consider customer service. How does the care staff interact with families and visitors? Can the staff members answer all the general questions you ask?

All staff should be able to:

1. Provide a basic tour of the facility.
2. Tell you the general pricing range.
3. Provide you with an activities calendar.
4. Tell you which department regulates them, e.g., Illinois Department of Public Health.
5. Show you where the displayed licenses are located.
6. Tell you whether or not there is a nurse on campus no matter when – 24 hours a day/seven days a week, 365 days a year.
7. Tell you the number of residents who live there.
8. Tell you how many caregivers are on staff.
9. Tell you how many nurses are on staff.

10. Tell you their emergency procedures and the prescribed course of actions in the case of elopements.
11. Tell you whether or not there is a weekend manager on duty and who that is.
12. Tell you how to reach the community "after hours" hours in case of a family or other emergency.

If the community specializes in memory care, the staff needs additional, ongoing training. Be sure to ask the Executive Director or the Resident Care Director when the last training took place, who conducted it, and, if possible, to see the training service outline or curriculum. In the past, when I conducted staff training, I would offer to email the PowerPoint presentation I used for training to the person inquiring. I believed this to be another opportunity to help educate consumers on dementia care and its associated care challenges.

4 WHO REGULATES SERVICES?

Throughout this book, I've offered you information about regulations. You may wonder why this information is so important and why I hammer on it so much. Sadly, because so many variables come into play when it comes to marketing and 'filling the building' -- getting folks to move in, that a less than scrupulous company may not pay much attention to those regulations. Whether the goal is to get a person to move in, or a more altruistic reason such as believing the person can be helped by their services, a tendency exists to bend those rules.

For example, in Illinois, residents in assisted living communities cannot require two people to assist them with getting up or transferring from bed to chair, or chair to commode. That regulation is often overlooked. If a person is overweight and truly does require two people to assist them, they are not acting appropriately. The dangers to the resident and to the staff in the event the person was to fall are not being considered.

State regulations are the "bible" for assisted and memory care communities. It is vital for you to visit your state department of public health's website and read the regulations BEFORE you begin your tours so you are better able ask the right questions while you learn about the community. For the sake of your loved one, especially if they are not accompanying you, be honest with the community's staff. In my experience, many situations have taken place because the family was in a crisis mode or desperate to find a place. Once the assessment occurred, and staff actually got to meet the potential resident, all the upfront work was for naught. The person was not accurately presented by the family member; precious time was wasted.

The regulations should always prevail. Be certain you understand at least these three components:

1. Residency requirements – these tell the community who they are able to accept
2. Training requirements – these are the state training expectations/standards required for the staff
3. Incident reporting requirements – this is the information the community must report to the state; they also include the contents of their policy and procedure protocol

5 HOW DO I **REALLY** KNOW WHAT'S GOING ON?

Have you ever watched the television show *Columbo* with Peter Falk? He would frequently say, "Oh, and just one more question?" Ask questions of a few different staff members. You should get very close to the same answer from each, but from their point of care. For example, the caregiver should give you an answer that relates to his/her role in patient care while a nurse would give you an answer that relates to his or her role.

Please visit communities at different hours of the day and on different days of the week. I love when a variety of family members come as well. You should know when the scheduled day to shower is, since that should be included in the Individualized Service Plan. Plan to visit that day, for example, but after the scheduled shower.

When your loved one first moves into a memory care community, you probably were instructed to stay away for between a week and 10 days. That gave the new resident a chance to bond with the caregiving staff and to create a routine.

After that, you were welcome to visit after dinner, before dinner, whenever. The point is for you to feel comfortable coming at any time so you can better understand the differences in staffing patterns and staff routines. That also is how you get to see and know what's going on at all times!

6 WHO SENT ME HERE AND WHY? DID THEY GET PAID TO SEND ME HERE?

I start this section with an apology to all the truly great, dedicated senior placement counselors out there who work for companies whose heart has remained true to the original business mission. There are quite a number of these companies like Care Patrol, Caring.com and A Place for Mom to mention a few. These are either very large organizations or franchises. Others are more local like Elderwerks, Senior Experts, and Graham & Graham. Then there are some strictly online companies like Senior Advisors.

All of the above have agreements with senior living companies to provide them with a move-in fee, which normally amounts to about being equal to one month's rent. Therefore, the short answer is yes, they have an incentive to send you to a particular place or places and will get paid if that's the place you move in to. The placement company then pays a percentage to the senior advisor through whom you connected -- or who typed in the location names and responded to your email.

When you began your search, if you are like me, you went directly to the internet. You began by typing 'senior living' or 'assisted living in Geneva,' then clicked on the first search result that popped up. When you did that, in fact, more than likely the result didn't link to the actual community, but to one of the services I mentioned earlier instead. Then, when you clicked again, you were connected to the service provider's website instead of to the community named in the title.

Once on that website, after you've answered a few questions, you either receive a phone call or your phone begins to ring off the hook. (I guess that little phrase really doesn't apply anymore, right? Off the hook? – oh, well, I'm old!! But you understand: you begin receiving a LOT of calls). What happened on the other end of your email is an automatic review of your answers by an area code 800/855/866/877 number. If the call is answered by someone who isn't local, that person will forward your info to the 20 or 30 'closest' communities who then receive you as a LEAD. By the way, that concept is called "spray and pray." The service sprays your info and prays that one of the folks who calls you back lures you in for a tour and makes you decide to move in. That is when the company gets paid a commission.

It seems rather bizarre considering all the nuances that accompany the search like: How many daily living activities do the person need assistance with? Is the person continent? How many meds do they take daily? Does the person wander? Do they exhibit behavioral issues? The list goes on and on.

What is the lesson to be learned here? Do not enter any contact information unless you are absolutely certain you have gotten to the community's website. Use a paper and pencil to jot down names of the places that seem to make sense for your loved one, then close all you internet windows and the research done regarding those communities.

There's no problem using a placement service, however it is best to do this only once you've gotten your feet wet and not only have researched the communities, but also the placement services. Are you becoming overwhelmed? Call me at 630-200-1149. I have no problem any questions you might have.

CHAPTER FIVE – CHECKLIST OF WHAT QUESTIONS YOU SHOULD ASK

1 DETAILS ABOUT THE COMPANY

When is big, too big? When you do your research and go directly to that company's website, don't just view the website's page tabs, dig deeper. Google the company's name. Visit SeniorHousingNews.com and learn what's happening in the company as a whole. What you learn about it **does** affect each community you view, tour and may be considering for your loved one.

For example, the company's website may indicate it is relatively small, owning only between 14 and 20 communities in total. You immediately think that this is great because they are all local, within the three or four contiguous states. This gives you a good feeling that 'help is nearby' should there be staffing shortage or turnover. However, when you then visit a senior business website, you note the company is about to be taken over, purchased or acquired by a much larger company based on one of the coasts. (This assumes that the person doing the research is from the Midwest). That changes the equation! What does that mean for the community you've just put on your short list?

In another scenario, when you go on the company's website and see the matrix that indicate the types of communities the company runs -- such as independent living, assisted living or memory care, and you realize that your chosen community is either the only one of its kind they operate or one of only a few memory care communities. Yikes! Consider this. Is this community a 'guinea pig' on which they will experiment to begin to enter into this level of care? These are some reasons by why you MUST go beyond the tour and do your research.

2 ABOUT THE MANAGEMENT COMPANY, WHICH MAY BE DIFFERENT THAN THE OWNERS

Since, more often than not, the management company is different than the company owners, you are lucky you if you can find a company that not only owns, but also manages, the community you choose.

Although I've mentioned it before, it bears repeating. Owners own the communities but often turn them over to management companies to oversee policies, and procedures and human resource assistance in return for a management fee.

When you tour the community, be sure to ask, "Do the owners also manage this business, or do they use a management firm manage it?" If you get a look similar to a dog staring at a fan, **RUN**.

3 WHO HANDLES WHAT?

It is very important to get the lay of the land, either prior to or once your loved one moves in; either way, this is critically important. You may be inclined to call the sales and marketing person you've worked with until now; however, you need to remember their role truly is just that – to make sales AND to market the facility. They do not have anything to do with operations, resident care, activities or dining services. They will graciously take your calls a few times then pass the information on to the appropriate person, but you truly need to go directly to the source.

Quite honestly, the one person you must get to know and create a working relationship with is the resident care director. This title may be different at different communities, but still functions the same way. This is the person who supervises the nurses and caregivers/CNAs and who has the most immediate impact on your loved one's health and day-to-day routine.

Always refer to the executive director for ANY matter, since every department reports to this position. If you do not get a response from resident care, call the executive director. If you're unsure about something in the contract, call the executive director. If you have any concerns about activities, dining services or outside services (described next), call the executive director. This person serves as the CEO/COO of the community.

If you are dissatisfied with the executive director, you can always place a call to that person's corporate office, which should be named in your contract. Similarly, your local state department of public health and the ombudsman's office should be listed as well. The latter two should be used for the most egregious situations, since a call to either of them will result in an on-site surveyor being sent to investigate the matter.

4 OUTSIDE SERVICES

Earlier, I spoke about outside services. Allow me to explain the concept. Depending on the type of community and its licensure, it may offer outside services such as home care, home health care, physician house calls, podiatry, dentistry, physical therapy, occupational therapy, speech therapy, wound care, and/or hospice. This list includes the most common outside service providers.

When you initially contracted with the community, that contract indicated what services are included as part of the monthly fee and which are not. For example, if your loved one moves into the community after being discharged from a hospital, chances are the person will, at least temporarily, need physical therapy and possibly a hospital bed. That physical therapist is considered an outside service provider. The hospital bed will be obtained when a physician's order is filled by a durable medical equipment company that rents such items, like hospital beds, oxygen tents, walkers and wheel chairs.

The services of a physical therapist will also be available based on a physician's order; however, before that order is filled, you should speak with the resident care director.

In a number of states, prior to a 'third party provider' rendering services to a community resident, the company providing services needs to be interviewed by the executive director. During that interview, a determination will be made as to whether or not the service company is in good standing with the state's licensing agency and has a certificate of liability insurance.

Therefore, while services and providers are always the choice of the residents and the person's family, the company chosen must be preapproved by the executive director. That is why the resident care director often will offer a few suggestions to you. Those suggestions will include companies which already have undergone the "vetting" process and enjoy an excellent reputation among other residents either living in that community or within the area.

5 STAFFING THE COMMUNITY – WHO ARE THE STAFF, WHAT DO THEY DO, HOW ARE THEY TRAINED?

Ask the executive director or the resident care director for the names, titles and roles of each staff member who works within the community. Find out if each is trained by more senior staff or by outside providers. Also find out what they are trained to do.

It doesn't hurt to Google the names you are given, or even to do a Facebook or LinkedIn search to learn more about them. Sadly, some people portray one persona while at their work place yet have another while in their private lives. This is not to say that social media comments they make are "wrong," as everyone is entitled to free speech and his own politics. However, you may find their language and vocabulary choices may prove unsettling.

For example, I have very strong views regarding abuse of any kind, be it towards seniors, children or animals, and I have been expressive at times. That kind of stance is different than the use of vulgar language and hateful statements.

6 TURNOVER -- WHAT DOES IT REALLY MEAN?

For a majority of my career, I have been a self-employed consultant working in the senior living industry. My expertise is increasing revenues and occupancy, and working with turnarounds and start-ups.

Turnarounds – This is a term used for taking underperforming companies and improving them in all facets of their operations; this often includes making staff adjustments. A recent company I turned around involved making major staff changes. For a number of reasons, I had to offer employees two options: improve their performance using a disciplined process, or leave to pursue other opportunities. When asked by the management company what the projected turnaround would be, I was dismayed to report a number of 50 percent. Imagine my shock when they responded that this percentage was their norm.

When a turnover occurs, there is less continuity, less tenured staff and more confusion. If the community goes through a 'turn around', this can be expected, but this should NOT be the norm.

CHAPTER SIX– IT SOUNDS LIKE MY LOVED ONE SHOULD MOVE IN

1 BUT WAIT -- THERE'S MORE

Once you and your family decide this is community is best suited for your loved one, what comes next? Before a move can actually take place, a few steps must be taken and decisions made. Normally covered in something called the "Move In Packet," the community should provide a list of necessary documents. These should at least include the contract; emergency information; a Do Not Resuscitate (DNR) order, if one exists; a list of current medications being taken; information about the last physician visit outcome; a 'lifetime story' -- a five to 10 page document that lists or describes the person's likes, dislikes, familial background, friends, any dogs or other pets, and so forth. All of this paperwork, once completed, is turned in -- not to the marketing director, but to the resident care director. The resident care director serves as executive director's clinical partner.

2 THE ASSESSMENT

Once your family has determined which community is best for your loved one and that a move will take place, an assessment is scheduled. This assessment may be done by the resident care director, the executive director or by one of the staff nurses and usually consists of six pages containing boxes to check. These boxes, with 'points' assigned to them, need to checked off as the professional walks through the physical, psycho-social and medical needs of the person. As an aside about these 'points based' forms, some places don't even know what the points mean. They have no ability to translate and fold the results of these points into their pricing model, nor do they have an updated form that takes into account, for example, problems that becoming more prevalent with dementia. Recently, I worked with a company that not only had no ability to include memory care into the pricing, but insisted on using an obsolete assessment tool despite the fact their pricing was 'all inclusive' based on the particular building into which the resident was going to live. This example is a priceless warning to be aware of the assessment tools being used. Ask for a copy on the spot and take a photo of each page so you have it for your records.

3 THE COSTS

Pricing models run the gamut ranging from the model where each component of care is customized, through one with an all-inclusive rate based on the part of the building or campus in which they are located. In this section, the focus is on assisted living and memory care communities because CCRCs have entrance fees and SNFs are covered, at least in part, by insurance plans such as Medicare and Medicaid.

Let's take a look at each.

Typically, there are four components that make up a final price.

a. Incontinence and level of incontinence – Who is supplying the product?
b. Medications -- What type(s) and how many are necessary? (As another word of advice, 97 year-old mom does not need to be taking calcium, fish oil or ginko biloba.)
c. Care needed -- How much assistance does the person actually need with daily activities like taking a shower? Do they need stand-by assistance, help getting into and out of the shower, or do they actually need someone to give them a shower?

d. Real estate – In what size room or apartment do they want to live in – and is it available for them? Is the available real estate a private suite, a companion, a studio, a one bedroom or a two bedroom?

Remember that assessment? Those points given add up; based on the final number shown, items a-c (listed above) will be predetermined for you. After that, you get to add more to the price of the real estate.

Another model is an all-inclusive pricing one which, merely based on real estate size, you are charged a monthly fee. A studio apartment runs around $5000, while a one bedroom runs around $6000, and so forth. The companies that use this pricing model believe that the care throughout the entire community balances out. This is a favorable approach.

Yet another pricing model is based on the 'area' or 'cottage' in which a person lives. Some communities have 'neighborhoods', 'wings', 'cottages' and other lovely monikers for separating the care types. The assumption that accompanies this pricing model is that if a loved one needs only 'basic' memory care, it's not as 'bad' as 'intermediate' and certainly not as bad as 'advanced.' Therefore, with all "things" being equal -- meaning room size, the price goes up per level. Again, this is not a bad idea, but, if the place you choose uses this, make certain that their assessment tool can translate into minutes of care spent on your loved one by the caregiver and/or nursing staff.

4 THE INDIVIDUALIZED SERVICE PLAN

Aside from the assessment, which -- for the memory care aspect of care is a bit "wonky" (defined as weird, unreliable and unfounded, although, according to some, better than nothing), there is something mentioned earlier called the Individualized Service Plan (ISP).

This ISP is a plan of care that will take into consideration all the aspects of your Lifetime Story, plus your loved one's likes and dislikes, along with other nuances that otherwise would fall through the cracks.

These include preferences such as the person wants to wear dentures to bed, has one or two hearing aids, prefers to watch activities rather than participate in them; all these should be incorporated into this ISP, which should be completed and signed by the person initiating it, the family member with whom it was reviewed and the Resident Care Director. This Resident Care Director should be, per the Illinois IDPH guidelines, a **Registered Nurse (RN), <u>not</u>** a Licensed Practical Nurse (LPN), nor a Licensed Vocational Nurse (LVN). Some communities do not hire RNs as their Resident Care Directors, so make certain that an RN is on staff and signs off on this plan. You will also need to obtain a copy of this document.

Bonus 2: 10 Warning Signs of Alzheimer's Disease and What to Do After you Learn the Diagnosis. Visit my website for your free download of this important document: _www.beyondtheseniorlivingtour.com_.

5 THE FAMILY STORY

Each community has a document they would like completed. This document normally consists of between five and 10 pages of questions that covers your loved one's distant past, recent past and present. While it may seem like a royal pain, especially at this time when you're just trying to figure out the best course of action, I have to stress: please do not, do not, **DO NOT** ignore this document. Why is this so important?

When completed correctly, then used correctly, this document actually can be a God-send for your loved one. (Some places just file it away, which is a major NO NO!) Because this questionnaire asks the family member who is acting as the responsible person of the resident, about favorite movies, music, hobbies, pets, religious beliefs, activities, friends, relatives, happy events, sad events and so on, it can help a caregiver bond, relate to and even help the resident adjust to the new assisted living environment.

I have seen some Life Stories that have dashes filled in where answers should be, while I have seen another Life Story -- lovingly and thoughtfully completed by a daughter -- that sat, hidden in the Resident's Care Chart. Of course, the concealed one never should have been hidden. It is the responsibility of the Resident Care Director and the Life Engagement Director -- also known as the Activity Director, to make certain this document lives, breathes and is readily accessible.

Keep a copy for yourself. Ask the staff how they are going to use this information, then make sure they do! When asked a question about your loved one, ask them if they found the answer in the person's Life Story.

This is a partnership. Neither party has all the right answers, but when you make certain you work as a team with the senior involved at its core, this makes all the difference in the world. In other words, when you operate with a senior-centric focus, you can't go wrong.

Although you may have read this before, it is important enough to bear significant repetition. Please keep in mind as you read this that my focus is **always** on the well-being of the senior resident, regardless of the level of care they require.

6 THE MEDICATIONS

In the assisted living world, medication programs can be an additional expense to the senior or to the person serving as his financial power of attorney. As mentioned earlier, some facilities charge a flat fee for medication administration programs, while others charge by the number of medications requiring administration. This means that between one and three medications equals one dollar value, while between four and eight medications equal a higher dollar value and so forth.

When you decide to make the move to assisted living, it is imperative that your loved one's primary care physician do a complete work-up on all medications, which includes everything being taken, whether prescribed, over-the-counter or as vitamins/supplements. This eliminates many that do not provide any real benefit to the senior. I realize that when a loved one begins to become forgetful – whether due to either a dementia diagnosis or a truly failing in memory -- the adult child often feels better if they can offer their mom or dad some sort of supplement. You, as the adult child, need to understand that this is for YOU, not for them. This is the reason why a physician work-up is critical. Only medications and supplements that will be beneficial should be available and offered.

Also keep in mind that swallowing becomes very difficult for someone experiencing the throes of dementia. I have witnessed one single, 45-minute medication administration, which had to be repeated twice over one 24-hour period. Aside from the fact that many of the medications and/or supplements administered provided no pharmacological value, the cost to you adds up in terms of administration and staff time. Also, the level of staff counts; if a nurse is involved, it will be more expensive than if a caregiver or CNA administers the medication. Be thankful you can provide the senior with such quality care and choices.

CHAPTER SEVEN – WHO'S GOING TO PAY FOR ALL THIS?

1 MANY OPTIONS

Skilled nursing facilities and supportive living facilities will ask a potential resident to complete a financial application before anyone can reside within its community. These two differently licensed facilities receive monies, in part, from either Medicare or Medicaid for care received, therefore it is imperative for them to know the potential resident's complete financial picture. Assisted living, memory care and CCRCs are almost always private pay, however private pay comes in many forms.

2 PRIVATE PAY

For assisted living and memory care, the monthly fee usually consists of two components, resident care and real estate. Depending on the cost of living in your corner of the world, that expense can range from $1,500 to $15,000 per month. Quite often, adult children are called in to help subsidize this expense. However, with the greatest generation being what it was, I often see mechanics, farmers and machinists paying from their life savings. God bless them! I shudder, while sitting with self-absorbed adult children, when they balk at the expense when they view this as their mother and/or father spending their inheritance on themselves. When you spend a lot of time in this business, nothing -- absolutely **nothing**, surprises you anymore. Thank goodness the 'good kids' far outweigh the others.

3 LONG TERM CARE INSURANCE

When my husband and I turned 50 and 54 respectively, we took the plunge and purchased long term care insurance through Genworth. A number of other companies offer this insurance as well, including John Hancock and William Penn. We also purchased the 'survivorship' option, which folds the deceased spouse's benefits into those of the surviving partner. Even through some lean times, we didn't cancel this policy.

I know some of the options may have changed a bit since we bought this policy, however, it can be a definite game-changer when you need assisted living care. My personal policy offers $230 per day toward that care, which, with some rough math, is approximately $6,100 per month, which will help subsidize that expense if and when it may be needed. The payments go directly to the community even though a bit of paperwork is involved: On a monthly basis, the business office manager must submit a 'claim,' amounting to just one additional bit of paper to file along with the monthly invoice.

If you are reading this and have relatively young parents, or you yourself are in your 50s, run -- don't wait -- to contact the nearest LTC insurance broker. You won't be sorry.

4 VETERANS AID AND ATTENDANCE PENSION

The Veterans Aid and Attendance Pension, sadly, is a largely unknown 'benefit' that you must know about. Interestingly, as I write this particular section, it is Memorial Day – a tribute to all those that paid the ultimate price for our freedom.

The official website page: http://www.benefits.va.gov/pension/curr ent_rates_veteran_pen.asp

I feel compelled to offer a tidbit from the VA page so you can see immediately that the very first bullet point is applicable in assisted living and or memory care.

"The Aid & Attendance (A & A) is the increased monthly pension amount may be added to your monthly pension amount if you meet one of the following conditions:

- You require the aid of another person to enable you to perform the personal functions required for living each day such as bathing, feeding, dressing, using the toilet, adjusting prosthetic devices, or protecting yourself from daily environmental hazards
- You are bedridden; your disability or disabilities require(s) that you remain in bed apart from any prescribed course of convalescence or treatment
- You are a patient in a nursing home due to mental or physical incapacity
- Your eyesight is limited to a visual acuity corrected to 5/200 or less in both eyes or your visual field concentric contraction is at 5 degrees or less"

You certainly can go through the VA to secure this benefit, however, considering the numerous twists and turns almost always involved, you might want to directly ask the assisted living community if they work with anyone in particular specifically for this service. Keep in mind that this depends on their financial qualifications. Also be aware that it is **illegal** for anyone to charge you to complete this application. That said, it is well worth the $500 sometimes charged by a wealth manager or financial advisor to perform a complete analysis of someone's finances to determine their eligibility for this pension. The professional will offer invaluable advice and correctly complete your application.

5 REVERSE MORTGAGES

Reverse mortgages may offer some assistance to you as you age or if one of the homeowners is going remain in the home. These mortgages apply mostly to those over 62 years of age who need money to help with home improvements in addition to paying for healthcare expenses.

These mortgages will allow you to convert part of the home's equity into cash without having to sell the home or be burdened by additional monthly expenses.

An excerpt from the Federal Trade Commission (FTC) states:

The Federal Trade Commission (FTC), the nation's consumer protection agency, wants you to understand how reverse mortgages work, the types of reverse mortgages available, and how to get the best deal.

With a "regular" mortgage, the mortgage holder makes monthly payments to the lender. In a "reverse" mortgage, you receive money from the lender and, generally, do not have to repay it for as long as you live in your home. The loan is repaid when you die, sell your home, or when the home is no longer your primary residence. The proceeds of a reverse mortgage generally are tax-free; many reverse mortgages have no income restrictions.

6 LIFE SETTLEMENT FUNDING / LIFE CARE FINANCIAL SERVICES

There is yet another option for paying for assisted living and memory care communities. That option is for the policy holder to sell his life insurance policy while still alive. The purchaser typically will be an institution, which will pay more for the policy than its cash value. The institutional investor will continue to pay on the policy and carry it for the remainder of the original policy holder's life time, considering this action an investment.

Another way to pay for these services ;mris by taking out a loan or establishing a line of credit with a company that allows up to six guarantors on the application, thus not placing the financial burden on one person.

Again, both of these options should be considered as a last resort. Unless you find someone that is very educated about these, you could be taking a huge risk.

For assistance, ask the assisted living community or contact me. My contact information is at the end of this book. Over the course of my entire 17 years of experience, I have encountered only two scrupulous sources!

CHAPTER EIGHT – SIGN HERE

1 WHAT DOES THAT CONTRACT **REALLY** SAY?

Contracts come in all lengths, ranging from between 10 pages and 50 pages. If you are convinced you want to move into a particular community (or have two possible contenders) ask for a blank copy of their contract, then read it carefully! It amazes me how much time one takes to plan for a wedding or a home purchase, yet, when it comes to reviewing this kind of contract and planning, very little time is taken. Often, making a commitment for this lifestyle change can take as little as two days!

This kind of contract often includes a lot of "legalese," and concepts that may not be clear, but the following are some of the most common components:

1. The rental apartment chosen and all that it entails; this includes its maintenance, entry,

cleaning, fees for damages, requirements for sub-leasing and what you can and cannot do in that apartment. It also includes its "appointments," such as handicapped shower, pull cords, window locks, door locks, and what will be their furnishings and yours

2. Specific fees for the apartment (real estate) and those for resident care, as well as their ability to increase rates and under which conditions they may do so. This will also define the frequency with which these fee increases may take place, along with what is refundable and what is not

3. The care level to be provided based on an assessment of the resident's actual physical and cognitive condition. It also includes any additional care that

can be provided and which policies pertain to these as well as how condition changes may effect the level of care, and when the facility can no longer care for the person. Details further include their ability to move the resident to a different setting

4. Termination for all causes, like:

   a. how and when you can cancel your contract and under what conditions this can be done -- with and without a 30 to 60 day written notice,

   b. how they can cancel the contract and for what for a variety of causes, namely inappropriate behavior on the part of the resident or family, and the facility's inability to

provide the appropriate
care required,

5. Who is financially responsible,
who is to be called and under
what circumstance?

6. who holds health care power of
attorney and who serves as the
financial power of attorney?

7. What is your recourse if you are
dissatisfied with the actions of
the organization's leadership
team? Usually the name and
contact information for the
specific state's department of
public health and the long term
care ombudsman is available in
the contract documents in the
state of Illinois. Other states
may vary in this regulation.

This contract document should be
mutually agreed upon. Therefore, if
something is questionable, you certainly
can ask to negotiate an amendment or
renegotiate that portion so it can be

eliminated completely from the contract. For example, this questionable item may be a 'nonrefundable' community fee or an arbitration agreement. Never agree to these arbitration terms -- particularly when working with a skilled nursing facility.

Consider this contract similar to a pre-nuptial agreement prior to marriage or your severance agreement prior to accepting a job offer. Make certain the 'sticky' points in question are resolved to your complete satisfaction BEFORE the move-in.

2 WHAT IF....?

A lot of things can happen at this point, prior to move-in. Planning ahead with your loved one, while optimal, is not actually the norm. Quite often an 'event' has moved this otherwise possible 'planned life event' into the crisis category, making it an immediate or short-term necessity.

When I changed jobs in the late '90s, making the shift from being a hospital administrator to serving as a senior living executive director, the average age of a resident who moved into our community was 82 -- and that was considered late. Over the course of the next two decades, home care, home health care, technology and the economy have caused this age to creep into the late 80s. Currently, the average is between 87 and 89.

Consider this scenario: A family makes the decision to move into an assisted living community. It pays the nonrefundable community fee -- which can anywhere from $1,500 to a $7000, if the community's policy is that the nonrefundable community fee is equal to a month's rent, and pays the first month's rent. The family purchases a twin bed and has a move-in date planned. Suddenly, mom – the intended resident -- falls, needs to be hospitalized, and, later, is transferred from the hospital to a skilled nursing facility for short term rehabilitation. Now begins the infamous 100 days. Suddenly, the skilled nursing facility tells the family mom cannot go into assisted living. The family must consider long term skilled nursing. What options are available then?

For the scenario above, you may change out any number of factors, like recurrent falls, mom becomes ill or the patient contracts pneumonia, wanders off into the night, or needs more care for some problem. By this time, the family has waited too long and now must skip directly to assisted living, memory care or skilled nursing! This happens all the time. What does the family do then?

Depending on the community, most likely, your paid fees will be refunded. Some communities will be gracious enough even to return the nonrefundable community fee, while others will not. Remember that contract?

3 CANCELLING

How do you put 17 years of experience between two covers and make certain you've provided all the information someone could need to make intelligent choices? As I probably mentioned earlier, the contract you signed contains language about cancelling. It really boils down to this: As in the case of skilled nursing, if your loved one must move out because the community no longer is able to provide the new level of care necessary, your contract is normally cancelled immediately. However, if your loved one decides to out because of dissatisfaction that cannot be resolved, then you need to provide a 30 to 60 day written notice that is specifically addressed and delivered to the executive director.

Regardless of whether a person has memory issues or not, caring for someone who requires daily living assistance is a difficult task. I offer kudos to all the caregivers who provide that care and do so with love and devotion, whether they are employed trained professionals or not. No person or company is perfect. Individuals must try to resolve the issues that arise. I will cover this in more depth shortly.

4 WHAT ARE THE NEXT STEPS

Once you've committed to the contract, this document specifies the location and type of apartment suite your loved one will move into as well as the level of care they are going to receive.

All the paperwork is reviewed by the various department heads to make sure everyone involved understands their role and involvement with this person once the resident moves in. 'What is their level of involvement?' you ask. Once it is determined that someone will move in, the department heads should collectively discuss the move-in so each understands how his or her department will interact. Are there any special needs or requests that they can or cannot accommodate?

For example, Dining Services will need to know if the person has special dietary needs or requirements. Is the person a vegan? Does the person need food mechanically softened? Are there certain foods they truly cannot tolerate? The activities area will need to know if the person is an active or passive participant. As an illustration of these, my dad, bless him, could not care less about football or baseball, but he loved to observe as others watched these games. He was a passive participant. On the other hand, my Uncle Russ would have climbed through the television while watching a game if he could. Russ was definitely an active participant.

In addition to learning these preferences, the caregiving staff needs to learn on which side the person prefers to receive assistance. The maintenance director should know if the person requires a cane, a walker, a wheelchair or other assistance in order to appropriately reconfigure the room for them, like install additional guard rails, and provide appropriate assistance to the family as furniture is moves into the room.

5 COMMUNICATION

I cannot stress this next point strongly enough. Everyone involved MUST communicate, or even over-communicate if necessary. Make certain that everyone is talking!

By this time, you as the concerned adult child should have conversations with the following team members:

> a. The **sales and marketing director (SMD)** – This may also be someone who has a similar

role who holds another title like community relations, resident advisor or sales counselor. These conversations must take place initially when you arrange for the tour and with the person who most likely conducted the tour. The SMD also will provide you with a contract to review. Often times, a 'move-in packet' that contains a list of all documents you must complete is available for your review and guidance.

b. The **move-in coordinator** – Few communities still have this position, but, if yours does, this is the person who will do just that -- coordinate your loved one's move into the facility and make sure all the appropriate paperwork is completed.

c. The **executive director** – Since this is the community's sales leader, this person should contact you by phone between 24 and 48 hours after your initial tour to follow up with you and find out if you have any other questions regarding the community. Questions about the contract, the rates, as well as other concerns should be directed to the executive director.

d. The **resident care director**, or **director of nursing** – This person should always be the executive director's clinical care counterpart. The nursing and caregiving teams report to the resident care director who, in turn, reports to the executive director. This person is responsible for completing and reviewing with you the Individualized Service Plan (IPS). This director also is responsible for both prescriptions for medications and durable medical equipment from hospital bed to floor mats, as well as the move-in paperwork as it pertains to the resident's care.

e. Other folks that you should meet soon after move-in include the activities director. (Remember that 'Life Time' story? The activities director is the person who will make that story come to life!) It also includes the dining service director – who oversees all the meals and nutritional needs for your loved one, and the maintenance director who fixes and makes repairs as well as takes responsibility for on-going attendance to the physical room itself.

From move-in day and continuing weekly over the course of the following month, ask for a sit-down meeting with the executive director and the resident care director. As I may have mentioned earlier, some places are darn close to perfect, but you still need a scheduled meeting to go over any minor, and definitely any major issues which have manifested since the move-in.

6 IF SOMETHING GOES WRONG

Something is going to 'go wrong' regardless of how well you plan to avoid any problems. Inevitably, what you consider as having 'gone wrong' most likely is a transitional issue that the community sees on a regular basis. My intent is not to minimize the impact of this move, but, if you can, remember tales of a baby's first day in school or pre-school. The teacher tells the parents it would be okay. The parent should just leave; the teacher had the situation under control. This is the same principle. So many scenarios exist that I could not possibly list them all; however, let me share with you a few common ones.

a. A **reluctant resident who had to move in** because he was not safe being at home alone. This person is grieving for the life he knew and is scared, not sure about what comes next. The person's nerves are frayed -- as are yours at this point. Your anxiety will not do them any good at this point. Trust the caregivers and their care team to help ease the reluctant resident into a routine. Share with both the executive director and resident care director any concerns you may have. Tell your loved one that, for the short term, you won't be available by phone. If he needs anything, he needs to speak with these same two people and they will get a message to you. Share your game plan with your siblings, then take a breath and rest. Both you and your loved one are in good hands.

b. **The "I want to go home" resident** is a common occurrence. Please, please, **please**! **Never** tell this person, "but you **are** home." For so many reasons and on so many levels, this is **not** the correct response. In fact, an explanation would probably require another book!

Typically, this resident has memory issues. The person is not sure why he is being 'sent away' or 'put into' a senior living community. The transition can be difficult for both you and your loved one. This resident will need to form a bond with the caregiver. In order for this to occur naturally, you may be asked to not visit for a week to 10 days. If this is the case, please make sure to create a game plan with the resident care director, as well as with the after-hours staff. Let them know that you will call when you feel the need -- even if the time is 2 a.m. Also, assure them they are to call you for any reason as at any time. This is not implying they should abdicate their responsibilities, such as medication administration, but lets them know you want to be informed about small 'incidents.'

Bonus 3: Visit my website and download a full presentation on Communicating with Dementia:
www.beyondtheseniorlivingtour.com.

I'd like to take a moment here to quickly address the subject of incidents. In Illinois, the Illinois Department of Public Health is adamant about 'Incident Reporting' and details which incidents they want reported to them as well as which incidents they do not need to hear about. Ask for a copy of the community's "Incident Reporting Policy and Procedure" manual. If you are told this is an internal document, ask for a synopsis and compare it with the regulations stated on the state's website.

CHAPTER NINE– MOVE IN DAY LOGISTICS

1 FURNITURE OR NO FURNITURE?

Once the move-in is planned and, if it is local, you certainly should be able to arrange to have the essential furniture delivered. When it comes to furniture, keep in mind that what fit into a seven or eight room house will not fit into a 500 square-foot studio apartment. This is especially true if a walker or, perhaps, a short- term wheelchair needs to be used or if another person must live in close proximity to assist the resident with movement and mobility. Additionally, think about this: In a small space, people tend not to look down, but straight ahead. As a result, low chairs, tables and items like knick-knacks often go unnoticed, heightening the fall risk.

Keep the furnishings pleasant, comfortable and simple. Instead of placing a television set on a small metal stand or table, if possible, mount it on the wall. Because this is a smaller space, it is best to avoid side tables, throw rugs, floor runners and items that may clutter the space.

Some communities offer short-term rental furniture for situations when the need is more urgent, or if someone is moving from out of town and needs additional items temporarily until there is time to purchase them.

2 DURABLE MEDICAL EQUIPMENT -- LIKE WHEELCHAIRS, WALKERS, CANES, HOYER LIFTS AND OTHER ESSENTIAL ITEMS

Just like a medication prescription, these items each require a physician's order to be filled. The resident care director can assist in coordinating these requests. Keep in mind, however, that Hoyer lifts are not allowed in settings other than skilled care.

3 WHO IS THERE TO MEET AND GREET?

When you and your loved one walk through the door on move-in day, the resident care director, along with one or two other key members of the community, should be there to greet you. Those individuals may include the executive director, the activity director, another person from the care staff, as well as a nurse or caregiver, and, possibly, the facility's maintenance director. The point is, you should never be left to your own devices. Someone should always be available to provide answers to your questions and offer guidance about care and logistics.

4 WHOSE IN CHARGE

Who holds the responsibility for what? Although the executive director is the CEO/COO of the community, at this point, the pivotal person is the resident care director (RCD). This person will discuss the care plan with you, make certain any and you either have in your possession all required medications or these are on their way from a pharmacy. The RCD will also be the one to facilitate obtaining any needed durable medical equipment, like a hospital bed, a wheelchair, a walker, oxygen machines and other required, helpful items. This team member also will provide introductions to the other nurses and caregivers who will be involved to provide a smooth transition process.

5 THAT FIRST NIGHT

I am not going to lie. The first night is usually the worst one for the family. Hopefully, you have faith that the care of your loved is in good hands -- the community's staff. Depending upon the level of care required, whether this is assisted or memory care, the first night may be difficult for your loved one as well. That is why it is imperative to establish positive relationships during the discovery and move-in process. You need to feel confident that what you are told is factual and you will be contacted only in the most urgent of situations.

That does not mean **you** cannot call them. Perhaps you've resigned yourself to having a sleepless night. By all means, in that instance, make that 2 a.m. phone call to the overnight nurse or lead caregiver. If your loved one moves into the memory care level, please do not provide them with a phone as this will confuse them. The person may do as one of my dear residents once did: She called 911 because she could not find her remote control. When the emergency service team arrived, as they must, they displayed a good sense of humor. My own mother would call the nurses' station at the skilled nursing facility to check in on 'Mrs. Letwaitis.' I once asked her why she did it; her answer was pretty simple. No one was telling her anything! Lesson learned.

6 VISITING

If you have the luxury of living close to the residential facility, you can visit at any hour you desire. In fact, it is a good practice to observe the routines of both the community and your loved one during the course of a day.

You do not need permission to visit, however, you must be sure to sign in– and OUT, especially if you are taking the person to a doctor's appointment, to lunch or anywhere else that is outside the building. Let the resident care staff know you are taking the person so any medication that needs to be administered can be given or a note made to administer the medication at a different time, pending a doctor's order.

CHAPTER TEN – RESOURCES

1 VISIT THE STATE REGULATIONS PAGE

In Illinois, in the state's regulations can be found on the Illinois Department of Public Health's website:

http://www.ilga.gov/commission/jcar/admincode/077/07700295sections.html

Most states offer a website or web page specifically pertaining to senior care that is filled with useful tidbits. I usually recommend you start there before you visit any other website. I suggest this because the state site won't steer you to a paid advertiser's link, which could ultimately get your contact information. Once the advertiser has that, they will start to badger you, encouraging you to use their business.

2 VETERANS ADMINISTRATION

The Veterans Administration (VA) website also is useful if your loved one served in the American armed forces. The VA lists available veterans' benefits, such as the Veterans Aid and Attendance pension, in addition to other useful links such as the pharmacy/medications plan.

http://www.benefits.va.gov/pension/curr ent_rates_veteran_pen.asp

3 PROFESSIONAL REFERRAL COMPANIES – WHO THESE ARE AND HOW THEY GET PAID

When I began in this industry, there was one referral company called A Place for Mom. Now, there are dozens of them -- some local, some national, some franchised and, others, offshoots of different service providers such as agencies on aging.

These professional referral companies get paid when you move into a community with which they contract to do business. The average is 100 percent of one month's rent and care charges. I will spare you my 'soap box' opinion about charging a community for 'care charges.' Let's just say this is an unpopular fee. However, I possibly stand alone on this issue. These referral services are free to you, except for the time you spend with them on the phone. Again, be judicious about providing your contact information. It will be used.

Of all the local referral companies out there, my favorite is Elderwerks, based in a northern suburb of Chicago. Its consultants have worked in this industry for quite a while, do an excellent job learning your needs, and do not 'spray' your information to many communities, and 'pray' that you will move into one of them. More information about them can be found at http://www.elderwerks.com/default.aspx

I have added this article excerpt written by Jennifer Prell, the founder and owner of Elderwerks, that nails it:

The Benefits of Using a Professional Referral Service

> The main role of a referral service is support. This service assists seniors, families and professionals in the search for senior housing, home care and professional services. The referral service consultants direct people to providers who best meet the senior's needs. Consultant referrals are based on factors that affect each senior's daily life. The factors may include, but are not limited to, the client's budget, medical history, personality, location requirements and the amenities preferred.

> Quality care is a major consideration in finding the best referral options for a loved one.

Personality is also important when considering referral options. As you research senior housing, consider your loved one's personality. Is he active and social? Does he enjoy being part of his community? Is he more on the quiet side? Is he religious? Does he enjoy gardening? All these are important to consider when making a decision. When you choose a community, make sure it is one that supports your loved one's normal lifestyle and one that will help him acclimate to his new community.

Senior communities have a standard array of services they offer. A good referral service consultant will be well-informed; that is her job. She can assist with information about the different levels of care, the meals, the building climate and staff ratios. This information is necessary when determining which community is appropriate for a loved one and his family.

Site visits to the communities being considered provide the knowledge necessary to make an informed decision. Visits provide an opportunity to become further informed about the activities, the meals, and the aesthetics of the building. The staff will introduce you to some of the residents, however guidelines and lists are available through most referral companies prior planning a tour.

As you consider a home care agency for assistance, conduct this interview as if you were hiring a new employee. What is the hourly or daily rate for service? What can we expect from the caregiver? What are the daily hours required for service? Does the referral agency conduct national background checks for and random drug tests on their employed caregivers?

When someone experiences specific issues such as Parkinson's disease, Multiple Sclerosis or dementia but prefers to "age-in-place" (at home), the consultant should be knowledgeable regarding referrals to the many of the best home services agencies. The consultant should know which agencies have additional caregiver education and which offer support for which specific diseases.

The consultant can assist with locating additional service providers like elder law attorneys, senior real estate specialists (SRES), realtors, financial advisors, senior move managers, home adaptability companies, emergency alert companies and experts in Veteran's Aid and Attendance.

As you begin to search for these and other options, a referral agency is a time-saver. The consultant's services are available at no charge to the client. These referral companies are funded by the providers in their networks. As part of their service, consultants must be objective and remain neutral regarding their recommendations.

4 VISIT THE COMPANY'S WEBSITE

Visit the company's website to read an overview of their mission, vision and services. The various pages of this site will also provide you with information about the other communities owned by this company, their news releases, programs and other events.

Most likely the site will not offer you any pricing information, as   many factors come into play before price can be determined. However, when you call, they should be able to offer you a ball park figure.

5 VISIT THE FACILITIES' WEBSITE

By visiting the community-specific website, you can learn about their management team, that team's philosophy and experience, as well as any upcoming events, pricing specials, and space availability.

6 CALL ME

When all else fails, call me – anytime. You can reach me at 630-200-1149 or by email at jo@beyondtheseniorlivingtour.com.

I sincerely hope this book has provided you with useful information to help you with your research, as well as a smile or two to break the tension and alleviate some of the stress this journey is bound to bring into your life.

It is important to gather the facts, do your research, remain open-minded to the suggestions of others, and -- above all else, trust your instincts. If it doesn't "feel" right, most likely it isn't. If it has great energy but doesn't 'look' the best, just squint a little to find the prize. Don't be distracted by a shiny new appearance. Find a company dedicated to protecting, engaging and loving their residents. I wish you all the best as you travel this adventure of a lifetime!

Bonus 4: When you go to the website, www.beyondtheseniorlivingtour.com, you can download a guide to the various communities/residences available.

This book, has hopefully, offered you some guidance through this difficult journey. Still need assistance? Call me:

Jo T. Letwaitis, CVW, CDP, LPACT

630-200-1149

www.ingramcontent.com/pod-product-compliance
Lightning Source LLC
Chambersburg PA
CBHW060541100426
42742CB00013B/2414